Organizational Agility
Unleashed

Getting Work Done in an Increasingly
Complex Digital World

Jim Grundner
Kimberly Andrikaitis
Bob Galen

Contents

Acknowledgments

Thanks to Sid Mitchener and the entire Vaco Raleigh team. You have created an environment in which we can help our growing client base deliver their products better and get stuff done!

I want to thank Brooke Forbes for her leadership, mentoring, and support. Beginning over ten years ago, you redefined organizational agility for me and demonstrated that developing trusting relationships is the foundation for successfully getting important work done. You have made me a better leader and a better person.

Bob also wishes to thank the patient and ongoing support of his wife Diane and his children in his agile journey. He also wants to thank his fur family members - Woody and Zoe. They all make the difference!

A smooth sea never made a skillful sailor. Kim is grateful for every turbulent wave and for the silent (and not so silent) mentors, coaches, and teachers who have helped me find my way. You know who you are. And I honor you.

Section 1

Enabling Business Agility and Getting Stuff Done

Why Do Businesses Struggle?

Does your organization seem to struggle to keep up with the demand for new products or product improvements or just flat out fall behind on every project in your portfolio?

Can you relate to the following statements?

- Our projects last longer than we think they should.

- When our projects are complete, they don't represent what we originally thought they would. In fact, they are substantially lacking.

- We seem to be continually disappointed with the results we are achieving for the dollars we are spending.

- We don't have sufficiently consistent practices and repeatable success seems elusive.

- We are willing to try almost any other approach to achieve better results.

Leaders and decision makers in company after company have told us they relate to these concerns. This book is an attempt to provide guidance and a map to overcome these seemingly universal business issues. Furthermore, we offer advice on how leaders can change their behaviors to build teams that continually overcome these basic challenges and become the high-performance foundation for excellence in this increasingly complex world of mobile computing, cloud-based applications, general technology acceleration, and rising budgets.

In this opening section, we explore five underlying foundations of organization agility:

1) Defining organizational agility.

2) Identifying and prioritizing what will receive focus and attention to get *done!*

3) Identifying what will *not* get any focus—*for now.*

4) Managing and limiting work in progress (WIP) at the portfolio level and in team operations to enable predictable completion.

5) Taming the chaos of a typical product portfolio.

Whatever business you are in, it likely involves more technology and data analytics than ever and is probably changing at an ever-accelerating pace. We hope the commonsense advice and approaches in this book will help you succeed in delighting customers and earning their loyalty.

Organizational Agility 101

There are many terms thrown about in the agile arena. Some are more widely known and used (Scrum and Kanban) and others are of more recent lineage (Scaled Agile Framework, DevOps, and agile transformations).

One of the most recent is this notion of *business agility* or *organizational agility*.

We have extensive experience with the core methods, agile practices, scaling frameworks, and agile leadership and culture, but we have found no community agreement on the definition of organizational agility. So we have decided to explore this topic further.

In the glossary on their website, the Agile Alliance defines business agility as "the ability of an organization to sense changes internally or externally and respond accordingly in order to deliver value to its customers." In their view, it is not a methodology or framework, but "a description of how an organization operates through embodying a specific type of growth mindset that is very similar to the agile mindset often described by members of the agile software development community."

According to the Business Agility Institute's website, "Business agility embraces change. Business agility changes how you think, how you work and the way you interact with people. This change is crucial at every level of the organization, from the operations floor to the C-Suite."

Both of these descriptions capture a piece of business agility, but we've come to think about business agility in the same way we came to understand DevOps or Software Development Operations. From our perspective, the theme of these discussions is that business agility directly connects everything the agile movement values—basic business drivers and the principles from the Agile Manifesto.

In a nutshell, the term is a bit misunderstood. It's not a separate thing. Instead, it's an aspect of the agile continuum, like Lean and DevOps.

As Steve Denning says, agile is about mindset. We believe organizational agility is also about mindset and likely a mindset shift—not just within the IT organization or the software product development organization but across your entire company.

For example, that's why Agile HR and Agile Marketing and how they play into business agility are so interesting to us. To achieve true organizational agility, you will need to develop new ways of thinking and working across the entire company.

Getting to Done

The traditional talking points of agile are that it is simple to understand and difficult to master given the required discipline and focus—why is that? Over the last 15 years as agile leaders in several different industries—financial services, health care, manufacturing, Software as a Service, and others—we have been impressed by the initial energy each firm puts into learning about agile methodology and their preferred pattern of implementation. Whether it's Scrum, Kanban, SAFe, or Spotify, everyone focuses on the success of the new and "better way of working."

At the same time, it is still important to get work *done* and seemingly an extraordinary struggle to do so.

In nearly every conversation, whether we are speaking with Product Owners, Scrum Masters, team members, or executives, we emphasize the need to focus on one simple four-letter word: *done*! Getting to done is all that matters. If you are not going to finish what you committed, why make commitments at all; in fact, why have an agile transformation at all? Successful agile, Scrum and other organizational agility approaches need *done* to occur to create predictability. Without the ability to predict our course based on data, our "better way of working" will not be better at all; instead, it will become the newest way to frustratingly not achieve either organizational or team goals.

Being done is exhilarating. In Scrum teams, who has not witnessed the energy and enthusiasm of those who complete all the work of the sprint—and conversely, the disappointment and frustration of missing the sprint goals? Since we know how good this success feels, why is it so hard to consistently get to done and celebrate the value we create for our customers?

Getting to done requires us to focus on the specific commitments of the sprint and honor the selection of the items in the sprint backlog. We cannot deviate from that focus or give energy or time to other distractions.

Some of the most significant challenges teams face are drop-in work, interruptions, and additional requests that are not part of the sprint plan. How can we best fend off these impediments to success?

- **Team members:** Be strong! Managing new requests falls to the Product Owner, so resist the temptation to do the work. Even if it will only take a few hours, those hours add up and steal from the sprint!

- **Product Owners and Scrum Masters:** Ask what makes this new request vital. Why does it override the previously identified priorities set in sprint planning? Build consensus around finishing what's been started and then review the new items for the next sprint.

- **Leadership team:** Support and trust the team's decision-making and, if needed, be the shield the team needs to execute their priority decisions.

- **Everyone, all the time:** Incorporate approaches that remind everyone of the need to honor the sprint commitment and the focus required to get to done!

Done feels so good for the team and enables greatness in organizations. It is a core tenet of agile methodology and creates a foundation that helps our customers come to trust us, believe in our words and actions, and come back for more!

What is holding you back from achieving *done*?

Scrum: The Art of What Not to Do

In his best-selling book *Scrum: The Art of Doing Twice the Work in Half the Time* (Random House, 2015), Jeff Sutherland describes the beauty, simplicity, and discipline of Scrum. It is a great read and describes how individuals, teams, and organizations can genuinely accelerate by selecting the highest priority work to complete and ignoring the rest of it. Although Scrum helps to prioritize and identify what *will* get done, it also, and more importantly, helps organizations and teams declare what **will not** get attention. And that is where we tend to run into trouble!

Organizations, teams, and people rush to the doors of Scrum like it's a New Year's resolution, hoping to get themselves in shape, to once and for all get some long-awaited projects and deliverables *done*. And, like those resolutions, about two months in the enthusiasm for Scrum has either disappeared entirely or ceased to resemble the initial desire for completed work and organizational fitness.

Here's an example of a client situation we can all relate to: Their portfolio requires about ten times the staff they currently employ. All the projects are a *must* for the coming year. Actual results show that the team's finished work typically represents about 50% of the total capacity of the workforce!

What is happening to the other 50% of capacity? Is this now Scrum: The Art of Doing Half the Work in Twice the Time? That seems entirely messed up, but unfortunately is more common than we think.

The key here is that while the portfolio of work to be done is being identified and declared, there is no matching organizational edict declaring which programs and work are **not** prioritized. Which should **not** get any attention or capacity.

Without that simple, clear communication, we can find some interesting behavior behind the scenes.

"Program Sponsors" whose work did not make the cut often open secret negotiations. We find them working with and pressuring team members to get a "little of this and a little of that . . . when they have a couple of available hours," maybe in exchange for a bagel or a doughnut!

This type of drain on the organization can build up. The capacity drain can be in the 30%–60% range—capacity that should have been dedicated to the work that was prioritized and selected. In one client, a group of nine Scrum teams found that a third of the team members were spending less than an hour a day on the sprint-selected work due to redirection requests!

For a moment, let's assume positive intent. Our jilted program sponsors may simply be aware of some pauses in prioritized work and are just looking to fill idle time, for the benefit of the entire team. That could be the case, or maybe not; it doesn't really matter, as it's a simple problem to solve.

As Scrum declares, we need clear, concise communication to everyone indicating what work will and will **not** receive attention, at least for now—not necessarily forever. We need to ensure that all available time and capacity is spent in the pursuit of the sprint commitments. This way, we position ourselves to receive the full benefit of fitness through organizational agility and discipline.

Let's all ask ourselves what we should *not* be doing.

Predictable Completion for Successful Customer Relationships

While learning, teaching, coaching, and exercising the discipline required to make the tough calls, sometimes we struggle. For agile to take hold in an organization, we must find a pattern that enables *predictable completion* of selected work. Predictability is the foundation of creating team and organizational accountability. It enables analytical conversations regarding when work will be complete, thus building mutual trust.

In a recent series of leadership discussions, one major topic was the accuracy of project information shared between the supplier organization and its customers. This organization, like many, does not have an excellent track record of delivering projects on the original timeline. The primary reason is simple—overcommitment.

To get to the bottom of this typical behavior pattern, we probed into the current state of customer trust. The question to the team was simple: What is your level of confidence in the answers you give regarding project and milestone completion? The response went round and round a bit. First, they answered "We hope it's correct." When asked to give that hope a percentage, they replied, "about 50% accurate." One more little push, just a little nudge: "Really?" The next and final answer was, "Well, probably around 20% confidence."

Let's think about that for a minute without being overly critical. The team does want their answer to be 100% accurate. They know it is a flawed answer. The black and white of it is that their answer is knowingly false, a misrepresentation of the truth—basically, a lie.

Before you jump on us, let's put ourselves in the buyer's shoes. After months and years of these hope-based answers, they likely don't trust any answer at all. They probably have zero confidence in what they hear; they hear it as a *lie*.

We submit to all reading: this is no way to build a long-standing business relationship. Think of any other relationship in your life in which you never believed what a person told you—nothing was trustworthy. How long did that relationship last? Have you basically dismissed that person from your life?

Let's apply that same potential for dismissal to our customer relationships. Are they potentially thinking of dismissing you and your company due to the same lack of trust? If so, what can you do to rebuild a foundation of transparency and trust?

The previous chapter discussed how to focus on committed work and resist redirection. Building on that, consider the following:

1. Understand the current flow of work in the sprint and use the completion analytics to baseline future planning—don't overcommit the sprint.

2. Create and adhere to work in progress (WIP) limits, with each team member having only one or two items in progress at any time.

3. Encourage team members hold each other fully accountable to the sprint goal and commitment.

4. Ensure the team uses the sprint retrospective to identify improvement methods and implement them.

By using these four simple steps, teams will evolve to higher degrees of predictable accuracy. This predictability will build on itself and create a transparent pattern of completed work, sharable with all customers, and likely resulting in improved trust!

Do you want to enable higher trust between your customers and yourself? Focus on improving your completion predictability!

Banishing Product Portfolio Chaos

The role of the Product Owner (PO) in agile is central to the overall success of the team. According to the *Scrum Guide*, "the Product Owner is responsible for maximizing the value of the product resulting from work of the Development Team."[1] To accomplish this, they work with stakeholders and the team to develop the product vision, strategy, and execution priority. The role is easily misunderstood if the person filling it is not well trained and coached.

On numerous occasions, a newly identified PO attends a certification class and then tries to tackle the daunting task of actually *being* the PO. When speaking with organizational agile leaders, we see several issues related to this:

- Belief that the PO is the be-all and end-all for product direction.
- POs who go it alone by setting vision, strategy, and priority by themselves.
- Loss of control over the work request and prioritization process.
- Growing belief that the voice of the stakeholders is just a suggestion.
- A need to improve PO understanding of agile and Scrum.

These and other PO misconceptions happen most frequently when superficial knowledge of agile or Scrum is combined with limited

---

1   Ken Schwaber and Jeff Sutherland, "The Scrum Guide: The Definitive Guide to Scrum; The Rules of the Game" (November 2017), 6, scrumguide.org

situational experience. We also see these issues when a PO has no mentor or well-versed PO community where they can share experiences. It also happens when the organization itself is new to Scrum and does not have enough overall expertise to execute correctly.

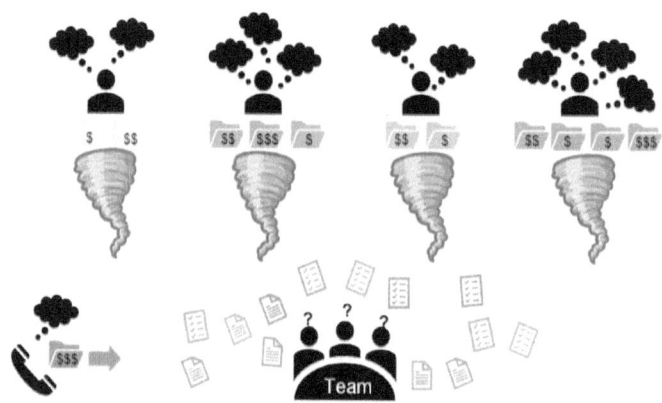

Figure 1. Poorly organized requests to the team result in conflict and chaos. This negatively impacts the amount of high-priority work completed.

The PO's role exists to manage through one of the most frequent problems for Scrum teams: too much demand and rapidly changing priorities. Figure 1 shows how organizations can get overwhelmed by conflicting needs. Teams lacking a stable, active PO can get stuck in the flow of requests. Stakeholders can complicate matters when they directly engage team members to push their personal agendas. Team members don't know how to react to these drop-in requests, and chaos reigns. These can be symptoms indicating a disconnect between PO and stakeholder priorities.

In this whirlwind model, chaos and churn are normal:

- Projects last longer than intended.
- Results do not meet expectations.

- Customers are dissatisfied.

- Practices are inconsistent.

A key PO role is to work with stakeholders to understand all stakeholder needs and priorities and negotiate a strategy everyone can support. In our experience, this negotiation can be tough. A typical pattern emerges where stakeholders dump all their requests on the PO and ask, "When will all work be done?" Frequently, stakeholders will comment that they only care about their own priority—the priority of the others is "not their problem."

This dynamic of conflicting stakeholder needs is the situation for which the PO is most needed. There is only one work team, and only so much capacity to go around. The team needs to be shielded from this chaos. The PO's role is to remind others of the greater good and negotiate a model that appropriately shares the team's capacity. If the PO cannot come to priority agreement with the stakeholders, no one's work gets done, and every customer suffers.

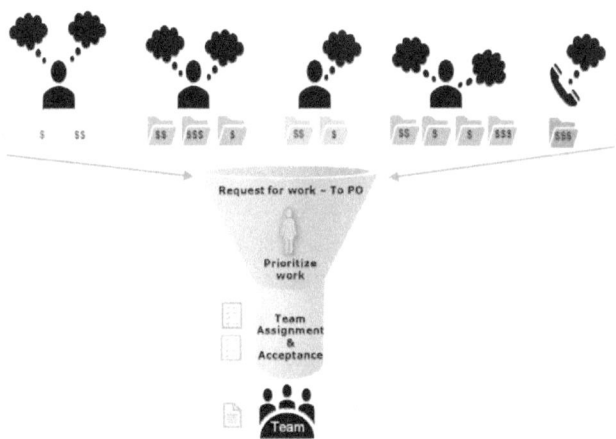

Figure 2. In an ideal work request process, the PO will collect stakeholder requests, negotiate priorities, and pass the filtered work items to the team in a way that balances everyone's needs.

Figure 2 shows an ideal PO work request process. The PO collects input and works with all stakeholder groups, negotiating to prioritize the team's work and ensure everyone's needs are met over time. It is vital that the PO work cooperatively with stakeholders to ensure full transparency in the prioritization of work. The sprint review is a terrific place to accomplish this.

When priorities are well organized, communicated, and executed, it benefits everyone:

- Projects are delivered on time.
- Customer expectations are met and often exceeded.
- Customers are satisfied with the results for the price paid.
- Practices are consistent.
- The team's approach to work is completely transparent.
- Customer loyalty improves.

POs have a difficult job. People in this role can feel as though they are on an island with nowhere to turn. Our path to success combines training, individual coaching, and the establishment of a mentored community of practice. When sponsoring conversations among a collective of POs, we find that the group members are often facing similar situations and experiences. By facilitating organized conversations, we help build a PO community where they can identify and share potential solutions. POs jointly learn the art of vision, strategy, priority, negotiation, and facilitation. These primary skills are amplified in a group setting, and strong bonds are built that will help them overcome new situational obstacles in the future— teaming to be great POs!

The PO role is tough and faces difficult situations daily. Learning how to deal with those challenges successfully is a team sport!

Section 2

Building Leadership Agility

Leadership Agility Goals

If executives adopting agile or Scrum aren't trying to empower teams, inspect and adapt, and handle emerging requirements, exactly what problems *are* they trying to solve? If you ask them, most senior leadership teams will describe real problems:

- We are constantly blowing past commitments; we need a way to fix that and do what we say we are going to do.

- We are putting poor quality products into the market and think agile can help.

- We need more transparency into ongoing work.

- We need more visibility into progress on the product.

- We need to get products into the market faster.

- We don't communicate very well; I hear agile can help us fix that.

- It costs too much to deliver software. We want to lower the cost to produce the product.

- We have way too much to do and not enough resources to get all the work done.

- Support work is constantly interrupting new product development.

This list is not surprising. Most leaders are looking for answers to problems like these, and we empathize with their search for solutions to these challenges. In decades of leading technology teams, we have both experienced all of them in a variety of forms and, frankly, it drove us up the wall at times.

But it's disappointing that executives are still seeing agile as a silver bullet that will fix complex, organizational, systemic problems. No mere framework or methodology has a chance of resolving these issues on its own. The apparent desire for a quick fix is discouraging.

There are no silver bullets or quick fixes to hard problems. Any solution will require the engagement of leadership, because most likely they are a part of the problem.

Scrum co-creator Ken Schwaber has often remarked during presentations or certification classes that Scrum gets blamed for creating problems when it's really shining a light on the problems. Leaders see the organizational issues and other systemic challenges. Team members find the impediments to their product delivery exposed. Project managers have to confront the flaws in their planning and estimates.

As Schwaber points out, once you see these problems, it's up to you to do something about them. Reflect, examine the root cause, and make a change. If you do, you'll improve. If you don't, Scrum will bring it to your attention again tomorrow. It can be very frustrating—particularly if you're looking for others to fix things for you.

Agility exposes challenges that all levels of the organization need to face and resolve—including the leadership team.

Leaders need to move away from silver bullet thinking towards truly partnering with their teams. They also need to take personal responsibility for learning about the methods and the mindset of agility and engaging with it and with their teams.

Finally, they need to look at the problems they have identified as more holistic and systemic in nature, as much their responsibility as their teams. Wouldn't it be great if leadership rolled up their sleeves alongside their teams and got to work on continuously improving things?

Organizational Agility Can Be Inconvenient

A good friend recently suggested an article or talk on "bad things that Scrum typically exposes." His list illustrated the sorts of things he was looking for:

1. Weak people (who managed to hide)
2. Time stolen (by people for pet projects),
3. Parkinson's Law (work expands to fill the time allotted)

Scrum exposes everything, so making such a list could be a long effort. But the following is a list of challenges, dysfunctions, and problems we typically see when organizations transform to Scrum.

This list is not intended to be exhaustive, but hopefully you will find it thought-provoking.

Scrum Transformation Usually Exposes That . . .

Leadership generally distrusts their teams. They distrust the teams' skills, their intentions. They distrust that their teams are accountable, responsible, and committed. That they are hardworking. That their estimates don't contain fluff, pad, or buffer. That they can work independently (without micromanagement).

Most organizations have established ineffective or dysfunctional metric systems. They measure pure output and not outcome. They align measurement with rewards and performance critique or with stack-ranking. Scrum exposes measurement that is about micromanagement and control—measurement that focuses on "trust, but verify."

There is a lack of teamwork. Instead of collaborating, individuals want to work only on their little piece and have narrow views of what they need to contribute. Team members show a lack of interest in any work beyond their own, considering a story done when their part is done. Scrum exposes team members who do not engage in whole-team planning in sprint planning or in whole-team estimation in backlog refinement. "I don't really care about that" is often heard in the "team" meetings.

Teams generally distrust their leaders. Teams too often distrust leaders' ability to make a decision—for example, choosing feature priority in backlogs. They do not trust that leaders care about the great people they've hired. They do not trust that the leaders trust them, which creates a "circle" of mistrust. Teams often don't hear about the leaders' vision, so they don't necessarily trust it when it comes, and they often don't trust leaders to be transparent and honest.

We have a general inability to estimate software and product development well. In a word, we still suck at it. We often get too far into the weeds too soon, trying to understand every detail. We want to break every user story down into 1- or 2-point stories, estimating only the development or the development-centric work and in such fine granularity that we lose the big picture. We task stories out too soon (before sprint planning) in an effort to understand everything and thinking that exhaustive planning is a guarantee for successful execution.

We continue to pursue the fool's errand of trying to define up-front requirements at 100% detail. We continue to assume that (written) requirements can be the sole communication method for customer needs. We continue to want to exchange text—email, text messages, tweets, and so on—rather than *talk* to each other. We also continue to forget that working code (visuals, prototypes, mock-ups, etc.) is one of the best ways to envision needs. We continue to get trapped by "That's not what I asked for" when we deliver our software. We continue to forget that *conversation* is the essence of communication.

We still have an affinity towards tools and processes (silver bullets) for solving our hardest problems. The first step for many agile transformations is, What tool do we buy?

Second step: What process do we pick?

Third step: What scaled framework do we pick?

In the fourth step, the managers draw an organization chart. In the fifth, managers form teams around the new org chart, with little training and little team engagement.

Then—Go, Be Agile!

Much later step: Why isn't this agile stuff working as promised?

Teams generally lack the ability to admit a failure *and* the ability to ask for help. We continue to assume that teams are perfect and don't make mistakes or don't tolerate mistakes. We continue to assume that failure is bad. We continue to reward loudness, brashness, extroverts, and reactive behavior over proactive thoughtfulness. We continue to look at experimentation, prototyping, exploration, and trying new approaches as a waste of time. We continue to expect learning to be done outside of our projects, as if we already know everything there is to know.

Organizations and teams always seem to bite off more than they can chew. We continue to make short shrift of backlog refinement, treating it as a wasteful activity. We succumb to business pressure and reduce our estimates and cut corners because of date constraints. We continue to make optimistic estimates even though history usually proves us wrong. We forget that "under-promise and overdeliver" is a very effective strategy.

We would rather rework something over and over than build it "right" the first time. We continue to implement the requirements, then be amazed when someone says "that's not what I wanted." We continue to rush into designs and code, only to have to redesign (or not) later. We continue to think that code completed is done. We continue to think that you can test in quality. We continue to wait until the last possible moment to show our 100% done work to our clients for "sign-off" and believe that lots of bugs are "inevitable."

Teams *always* know who the best (and worst) performers are on the team. Managers continue to think that they are the best judges of who performs well in teams and rarely ask their teams who is leaping tall buildings. Managers view individual performance over team performance. Managers are usually uncomfortable engaging in their agile team ceremonies and observing to gather performance information. They continually refuse to change their minds on overall performance (team, individual, etc.) based on new information.

Teams aren't the primary challenge when "going agile." Organizational leadership and culture are the primary impediment. We continue to focus on training the teams and coaching the teams, while assuming that managers and leadership understand agile principles and approaches, or allowing them to simply say they do. We continue to use the preexisting management approaches (and metrics) for leading our agile teams. Then we continue to wonder why agile transformation is so hard and blame it on those pesky teams.

Change is hard! Organizational change is hard. You need champions and leaders who inspire, envision, and lead the efforts. Everyone is involved in an agile transformation—no one is exempt—and it requires continuous effort and learning. It requires steady leadership that continues to push agility when the going is easy and hard. Asking for help is a sign of strength, not weakness, and external agile coaches are part of the change, so don't go it alone.

*   *   *

Hopefully, this list inspires you to think of anti-patterns you might recognize in your own agile transformation—not to make you feel intimidated or overwhelmed, but to encourage you to face them as a team.

Start with Yes!

Do you recall the Jim Carrey movie *Yes Man?* In it, an overbearing motivational speaker extracts a promise from Carrey's character that he will say yes to everything—every question, every opportunity, every inquiry.

The point is somewhat captured in the agile posture of "Yes, and . . ." that many coaches subscribe to.

Traditional leaders who are moving towards agile methods typically take a class or workshop to gain a cursory understanding of agility. Some even take more advanced workshops focused on the leadership shift.

But it takes a lot to get agile leadership into your DNA—much more than any class, workshop, or simulation can provide. It requires practice, particularly around the following:

- Empowering and challenging your teams
- Extending trust—*really* extending it without "trust, but verify"
- Allowing and encouraging teams to solve their own problems
- Supporting the team's ideas, no matter how far-fetched
- Providing all the resources they need and ask for
- Resolving team impediments and escalations

Not to mention generally guiding and supporting those great folks you've hired in kicking butt and delivering value for your customers, all the while having fun doing it.

Another way to look at leadership is to become a servant to the team. Say yes to becoming a resource to help them get their work completed. Mentally switch roles with them and know that success comes when you work for them, instead of the other way around.

It takes doing something 14 days in a row to make it a habit. We're going to double that timeframe, because this challenge will be extraordinarily hard for most leaders.

Say yes to everything your teams ask for 30 days.

- Say yes to requests.
- Say yes to ideas and proposals.
- Say yes to issues that are escalated to you.
- Say yes to estimates and plans.
- Say yes to designs.
- Say yes to requests for help or assistance.
- Say yes to *everything* for 30 days!

After it's over, reflect on what happened from a leadership perspective.

- How did it feel?
- How did your teams respond (in the beginning and over time)?
- Did the world end? Did catastrophes occur?
- What were the ultimate results?
- More importantly, what did you learn? What adjustments might you make to your leadership style?

Always Assume Positive Intent

"The team just doesn't have a sense of urgency."

Have you ever uttered those words? Or felt the frustration of this preconceived notion? Have you ever wondered why your teams aren't performing to your expectations? You question whether they just lack passion, or simply don't care, or maybe they just aren't into their jobs. Are team members just phoning it in?

Maybe. Or maybe . . .

Maybe they don't have the skills necessary to perform the work, and need to be taught.

Maybe they can't focus due to getting pulled in multiple, conflicting directions.

Maybe the user stories are too large, too complex, or too bulky to finish within a sprint.

Maybe they are working on outdated laptops, with severe performance issues, and they literally cannot speed up their process.

Maybe they don't understand the expectations due to language, cultural, time zone, or physical barriers.

Or perhaps, maybe, the sense of urgency was never adequately conveyed because they don't know *why* they're doing the work.

How would asking curiosity-based questions change our internal narrative? The dynamics of our relationships? What if we proceeded based on *curiosity*, rather than secretly fuming from a place of scrutiny and distrust?

Assuming positive intent is the first step towards strengthening our bonds with our teams, rather than destroying them based on false presumptions.

Try assuming positive intent as a personal experiment. For 15–20 days, stop to reflect whenever you feel conflicted regarding intent. Each time, try assuming the positive. Afterwards, reflect on your experience: Did your relationships shift? Did you gain insight about yourself, your team members, or the process? Did you find yourself responding from a place of empathy or concern? How did it feel to assume positive intent—did you feel less frustrated and gain empathy?

This is just one step we can take to strengthen our relationships and build in psychological safety, not only at work but in our personal lives as well.

Stay positive! Stay curious!

With All Due Respect: The Art of Giving Great Feedback

Giving feedback is one of our favorite aspects of the agile methods, but it's easy to give ineffective feedback. Lately, we've heard agile team members start their feedback with things like:

- No offense, but . . .

- I don't want to rain on your parade, but . . .

- I don't mean to be negative, but . . .

- I don't mean to criticize, but . . .

- I don't mean for you to take this the wrong way, but . . .

Clearly none of these prefaces are honest, nor do they effectively mask the intent of the person giving critical feedback. Often, they only provide a useless buffer.

Everyone in agile instances should be more thoughtful with their feedback. Remember, your job isn't simply to say it, it's to say it in such a way that it's effectively received and drives the changes you are trying to influence.

Effective feedback should be measured by the outcomes that it inspires, not by the simple fact that it was said.

Here are a few other considerations to think about before you give someone feedback in your next agile ceremony.

- Consider whether you are prepared to give the feedback, or are just reacting. Often, reacting in the heat of the moment is a bad idea. Give yourself time to be thoughtful about what you're going to say and how you're going to say it. In other words, prepare!

- Consider the timing. We've all heard that giving feedback in the moment is best, so don't wait too long. But sometimes, immediate feedback can be received poorly. Take a moment, take a breath, and collect your thoughts. This can help with effective delivery and temper any negative emotions that may exist.

- Consider your context. Do you know the team or the person well? Have they received harsh or constructive feedback? Do they do well or struggle with it? Was it recent? Have they received similar feedback to what you're about to give them?

- Consider the environment. Is it public, private, or something in between? Where you give the feedback is almost as important as when you give it. More private situations allow you to limit the exposure to those that need to receive the feedback.

- Consider the medium. Face-to-face is best. In many situations these days, feedback is given by email, text, or some other documentation-based mechanism. It might be old-fashioned, but I'm a firm believer in providing feedback face-to-face so you can see the body language of the receiver and adjust your message according to how it's being received. That's impossible to do via email.

- Consider the recipient. Someone once told me to always ask first. If the answer is no, now isn't the time, then respect that. Remember, timing is everything. Feedback should be timed appropriately for the giver *and* the receiver.

This applies to all sorts of feedback. For example, have you ever received an email reply that was clearly sent too soon? One where you could tell the sender had reacted to something in the email and said things that (you imagine) they now regret?

You probably have. We have too. In fact, we've been on the sending side of some of those messages. Try holding onto your messages and not reacting too quickly. We often wait for a day to send replies. What a difference a day makes in crafting feedback!

So, "with all due respect," we encourage you to be careful and thoughtful in giving feedback within our agile teams. But indeed, please give it!

Why Is Trusting So Hard?

The notion of trust is a sort of a chicken and egg problem in many agile teams:

- Do you give the team your trust as an organization, or do they have to earn it over time?

- If they make a mistake or miss a commitment, do they immediately lose your trust and then have to start earning it again?

- Is trust reciprocal? That is, does the organization need to gain the trust of the team? And if so, how does that work?

Quite a few leaders who are "going agile" have been talking about earning trust lately. Their attitude is along the lines of "I'll try this agile stuff and see how it goes. If it and the teams earn my trust, then I'll support it. But essentially, I don't believe in this stuff and you must show me that it works."

The harsh reality is that many leaders do not trust their teams. The other, even harsher, reality is that the teams know they are untrusted. They see evidence in a variety of actions and behaviors that speak far louder than words:

- Leaders who challenge the team's plans and estimates too harshly, always trying to influence lower estimates.

- Leaders who fail to understand previous, in-process commitments and overwhelm the team with more work than they can do.

- Leaders who say things about the team that they won't say to their faces.

These are just a handful of the behaviors we frequently witness.

Usually when a manager is confronted about this behavior, the response is that the teams have not yet earned the organization's trust. This line of defense feels like a smoke screen to enable a distrustful culture.

Why should leaders start by giving trust? To change an inherently distrustful culture. Leaders must set the example and **trust first**.

Once managers show that they can be trusted to trust, the teams will pay attention. They'll get rid of their own baggage and over time will start coming around to believe and trust leadership.

True trust, deep trust, and *real* trust can't be measured when things are going well. When things are going poorly and the pressure is on from every direction, do you still trust your teams? That's the true measure of your commitment to trust.

Leaders sometimes speak of "losing trust" in a team. Perhaps we should change the word to *confidence* in some instances. If a team is going through difficulty, you might lose confidence in their ability to deliver on their commitments. You should still trust that they're professionals and doing the best they can; they're just hitting a rough patch. Trust that they're self-aware enough to reflect on their difficulties and work hard on improving.

Most organizations hire good people. They have solid hiring practices and engage trustworthy professionals. Then they bring them into the organization and limit their capabilities and results by withholding trust.

Here is an inspiring perspective on trust from Jeff Nielsen of 3Pillar Global, from an interview with AgileConnections. "The best thing you can do is make a promise and keep it. And once you do that several times in a row, that becomes the new story." Repeatedly delivering on a commitment "goes a long way in building trust," even if the commitment is relatively small, like being on time to a meeting.[2]

"The other key aspect of trust," he says, "is trusting that someone else is considering your interest. It's great to have someone that always does what they say they will do, and it's easy to trust that kind of person. It's even better," he goes on, if you can trust that someone "will do what they say they're going to do and keep your interest in mind as they do that."

A lot of what Nielsen talks about in this interview revolves around making commitments and staying true to your commitments. Can we all agree that consistently living up to what you promise builds a strong foundation for trust to exist?

We always coach leaders (managers, directors, senior leadership) that they need to extend trust in the beginning of their agile journey. If they take the posture that the teams must earn trust and that they will verify it, performance will be undermined.

Do you extend trust indefinitely without results or reciprocal actions? No. But you extend it long enough for your teams to understand that things have changed, you're trying, and they indeed have your trust. In other words, that they're empowered to be self-directed and need to take ownership and be held accountable for the results.

"Trust, but verify" is a common attitude, but we all need to stop saying this—or even thinking it. If you need to verify, then you haven't let go and you don't trust your team. Period. You may think of this as a positive, trusting posture, but it's not.

Keep in mind that agility, almost by definition, is "self-verifying." As a leader, you can attend daily stand-ups, refinement meetings, planning

---

2 Cameron Philipp-Edmonds, "The Importance of Trust in Agile: An Interview with Jeff Nielsen," *AgileConnection*, TechWell, June 10, 2014, https://www. agileconnection.com/interview/importance-trust-agile-interview-jeff-nielsen.

meetings, and certainly the sprint demo. You'll gain a tremendous amount of "verification information" from your team.

As leaders we often have the false view that the team is there to "serve" us. We should flip that narrative in our thoughts and actions. Leaders should focus on gaining the teams' trust by demonstrating they are there to serve the teams' needs to achieve success.

Leaders need to cultivate a mindset of 360-degree trust.

- Do the teams trust our vision and goal setting?

- Do they trust our business sense and value-based prioritization?

- Do they trust our general decision-making and balanced view?

- Do they trust that we are fair and reasoned?

- Do they trust that we are trustworthy and have strength of character?

- Do we do what we say and say what we do?

Leaders would likely benefit from an 80:20 focus on trust: 80% of their attention on gaining their teams' trust and 20% on trusting their teams. That trust juxtaposition would serve all of us well.

It is probably safe to say that we don't explore developing trust often enough in our pursuit of achieving organizational agility. Why is this? It is clearly an uncomfortable topic, but that does not excuse its lack of attention by leaders.

Clearly, nobody will easily admit they don't trust another person in their working relationships. Too often, we look at it as a binary thing: either we trust (good) or we don't trust (bad). But there are many degrees of trust—and perhaps confidence.

Why don't we change that narrative and start every relationship with built-in trust? Much like assuming positive intent, leading with trust should create a powerful foundation for the teams to be successful.

Section 3

Building High-Performance Teams

Interviewing and Building Teams

A few years ago, I had the good fortune to work with a leader who constantly was thinking of innovative ways to build teams. He specialized in ways to identify, interview, and hire new team members.

At the time, this organization was growing rapidly, so it seemed as if we were always interviewing to meet the growing staffing demands. We went through a period where no candidates seemed to pass our screening process. It was frustrating because the recruiters kept saying they were sending us qualified candidates, but the team-based interviews would just chew them up.

We felt like we were searching for unicorns—people with a broad spectrum of advanced skills—and we were not finding anyone who met our stringent requirements.

Given this situation, our leadership team changed our interviewing approach. We called our new philosophy "the Three A's" and emphasized that we had to evaluate these qualities in this order:

1. Attitude
2. Aptitude
3. Ability

Attitude is an intangible characteristic, but it was our most important hiring factor. We were looking for candidates who were optimistic, good team players, open-minded, self-aware, and mature.

We spent a lot of time with each other on our teams, so it was important to hire folks we would like to be with every day. People who blended into our culture well and were (largely) a joy to work with.

The key to **aptitude** was adaptability and learning potential. We focused on trying to understand each candidate's career path and how many things they had learned along the way. We looked for learning on the job and for how much responsibility they had taken for their own continuous learning. Were they curious? How did they approach the unknown?

Another key here was flexibility in their jobs. For example, we would ask a software developer how they felt about helping out with testing in their agile teams.

The final criterion was **ability**. Here we were looking for the candidate's raw experience and skill level. This is where we had previously focused all our attention, looking for unicorns.

Instead, we made this the least important of our criteria. Sure, we were looking for folks who had skills, but we felt that an individual with mid-level skills who had a great attitude and aptitude could be trained by our other great hires. And we learned in practice that this was true.

We had also been stuck on degrees in our recruiting. For example, you had to have a hard computer science or engineering degree to be considered, and it had to come from a top-notch engineering school like Carnegie Mellon or Virginia Tech.

As we changed our philosophy, this mattered less and less. One software developer candidate had a PhD in Music and was a member of a jazz ensemble. Historically, we would never have considered him. Using our new philosophy, we decided to hire him as a candidate with outstanding potential. Long story short, he joined us and blew us all away.

Our most senior leader was very good about reinforcing the new recruiting approach and philosophy. We were so entrenched in our previous approaches that a one-time delivery would have just "bounced off" everyone. So he didn't do that.

Instead, over time, he continually reinforced this change in large meetings, management-level meetings, and hallway conversations. Every relevant chance he could find, he would make the case for and remind folks of our Three A's strategy. He was doggedly persistent, patient, and consistent in sharing his goals for how we built our teams.

We were a committed agile (Scrum) organization, and this strategy for putting people first helped us create high-performance agile teams. But the real proof in our recruiting strategy, agile team development, and personal development was the journeys of our team members. Former colleagues from this organization speak about their time at this company as being one of the best jobs of their careers. They also seem to show tremendous professional growth and have all gone on to become great leaders themselves.

For leaders who aspire to build great agile teams and who are ultimately measured by each individual's successful long-term growth, the Three A's strategy is an incredibly sound one.

Building Teams

There is always plenty of interest in the dynamics of building agile organizations from a structural point of view.

But you don't create a high-performance agile organization using the defined org chart. Managers don't do it; neither do VPs or directors.

We set the stage, but the teams are the ones that create the organization. We don't have to optimize the organizational structure for every technical hurdle or risk or create a structure that perfectly balances skill sets and experience across all functional roles.

That's good news because it's nearly impossible to do that perfectly anyway.

We simply pull together a reasonable approach to structure and try to be as balanced as we can. Then we form the teams, provide some intelligent constraints, identify the outcomes we desire, and get out of their way, allowing them to grow and perform. It's as simple as that!

Over time, the teams learn and adapt and will suggest changes. We need to be supportive of their insights and learning and help them adjust structures for increased productivity, quality, and value-based delivery.

What follows is some guidance that comes from our experience "building" agile organizations. These aren't guaranteed rules, just things that have been helpful in setting the stage and enabling great agile teams to emerge.

Creating Self-Directed, Cross-Functional Teams

First, we have a responsibility to create self-directed teams. These are teams that are composed of a cross section of the skills and capabilities needed to implement their product backlogs—the work the teams will be given.

Beyond raw technical skills, experience also comes into play, especially from a business domain perspective. For example, try to place a more experienced engineer on each Scrum team—someone who has technical chops in the areas the team will be exploring. They might be referred to as a Technical Lead or Team Lead or a similar title, but the title isn't what's important. What's important is having a seasoned and experienced person on each team.

Of course, there will always be constraints. You might not have a skill set in-house or enough testers to go around. Our job as leaders is to wisely distribute the skills we do have in a fair and balanced way across a set of teams. We should make this process as transparent as possible to our teams, and if we have discovered gaps, we need to share our intentions and plans to fill those gaps over time.

One way to handle these short-term gaps is by splitting or sharing folks across teams. While it's not optimal, sometimes it's all we can do.

Finally, vet your proposed organization alignment and team structures with your team members. They'll ask questions, provide feedback, and raise issues you never considered. It will help you improve your initial team alignment. But beyond that, it will increase the teams' understanding of your choices and help create buy-in when you roll out your teams.

Distributed Teams

Let's make one thing perfectly clear: distributed teams are hard. They're out of the "sweet spot" of agile team construction (co-located and cross-functional teams).

Does that mean you can't make agile approaches work in distributed teams? Of course not. But it does mean that you should adjust your approach.

As often as possible, keep teams entirely together, even if that means you have to make some compromises on skill set, budget, or strategy.

If you do have to distribute a team, try to do it intelligently. For example, try to keep the developers together in the same place (or the testers) so they can have a modicum of teamwork. Another approach is putting everyone on video so they can hear and see each other.

Invest in tooling that will foster collaboration: development tools, agile tools, video conferencing, interactive sites, and so on. Let your teams explore and define their needs and respond to their requests.

If you must have a Scrum Master or Product Owner who is separated from their team, consider asking someone on the team to serve as a local liaison for the remote person.

Invest in getting the entire team together at the beginning of the project (charter/initiation). Do some training and team building and run the first sprint as a localized team. This will pay huge dividends over the long term.

Make sure you allocate funding for frequent team member travel between your different sites. Quarterly or bimonthly travel can be very effective.

And most importantly, coach your teams to invest in solid agile teamwork and collaboration practices no matter the distance. For example, the team needs to commit to daily stand-ups, backlog refinement, and sprint planning *as a team* no matter how challenging the time zones and cultural differences are.

You'll get your best results with co-located, self-directed, cross-functional agile teams, so whenever possible, consolidate your distributed organization towards this goal. In other words, be relentless about moving your teams closer together over time.

Part-Time Team Membership

Can you have part-time team members on a solid agile team? It depends, but try to avoid the situation as much as possible.

For example, having everyone on a given team at 50% availability is a terrible idea. Clearly, some team members need to be fully engaged and focused on the tasks at hand.

But what about a part-time performance testing person on a team? Maybe. Or a part-time technical writer? Again, it might make sense.

There are two reasons to have shared or part-time people assigned to Scrum or agile teams. First, they might have specialized skills that aren't needed full time on every team. A good example of this would be a technical writer. The second reason is the ebb and flow of work for some specialized folks.

For example, one organization we know made the mistake of placing UX folks full time across a group of Scrum teams. They couldn't effectively deliver on many aspects of their jobs because the focus of the teams was on feature execution and the UX folks needed some time for design "look ahead" and research. Connecting the UX folks to the teams part time when needed created a much more effective balance.

The Scrum Master Role

People sometimes ask if a Scrum Master is absolutely necessary on the team.

The short answer is yes.

We recommend that organizations find a Scrum Master–like person (a coach) for new instances of Kanban. This role, if staffed with the right person and done well, is a game changer in accelerating new agile adoptions.

Does the Scrum Master need to be certified? Perhaps not, but they need experience in lieu of (or in addition to) certification.

Can you do a "time share" with an internal team member as a Scrum Master? Sure, you can do anything you wish. But part-time or multitasked Scrum Masters aren't a good idea. We recommend investment in professional and experienced Scrum Masters. If funding is running short, consider overloading them a bit with two teams each.

Not finding, hiring, and training Scrum Masters in your organization is one of the most shortsighted decisions you can make when you're planning for your agile transformation: a penny-wise and pound-foolish mistake.

And taking that approach with Product Owners is potentially even more dangerous.

Team Size

When considering team size, the general Scrum advice is to have teams of seven, plus or minus two. This is sound advice.

Even within that range, smaller is often better. For example, teams of five or six people seem to be a sweet spot from a productivity and efficiency perspective.

One growth organization we worked with provides an interesting case study. They were growing as a company and had a habit of growing their Scrum teams with new hires; when the teams reached a level of knowledge and understanding, it was split in two. There was a deep belief in the company that this approach was sound—like pair programming, except for teams.

At the time of this case, one team had grown to twelve people. This team was apparently working really well, but it was large. However, before the planned split could happen naturally, a business priority shift occurred, and they expedited the split to two teams of six to double focus on another business initiative.

Interestingly, in the original team's first sprint, their velocity only took a marginal impact—one or two points. The team had literally been reduced by half, but their velocity didn't change. The smaller team size simplified communication and increased their effectiveness—to the point where half the team was nearly as productive as the larger group.

Try to keep teams as small as possible while still including the requisite skills to get the job done.

Team Cohesion

Some organizations move team members around from team to team as if they're playing musical chairs. There's always a reason for it. Often it's something like, "This project is late so we're assigning more team members for the next thirty days to recover it." The people are treated like commodities or as if they're fungible. They're not, but that doesn't seem stop us from treating them as if they were.

The impact of this can be severe, especially within agile teams. Leadership in an agile organization should look to minimize disruption to the cohesiveness of the teams. Well-formed, high-performance teams are a critical aspect of the delivery proposition. It takes so much time to build a cohesive team that we shouldn't think of changing it willy-nilly.

Try to keep your teams together as long as they're healthy and performing, even when the business pressure is on.

Sitting Together

There is an incredible amount of debate surrounding how to set up team areas for collaboration. One extreme is to keep team members in cubes or offices that separate individuals and impede teamwork and collaboration. The other extreme seems to be throwing everyone into a large room at a single table.

Both approaches have a grain of truth in them, and the goal should be somewhere in between. A relatively old convention or tactic within the Extreme Programming community called "Caves & Commons" makes the point well. It implies that agile teams need both "caves" for private, individual immersion and work and "commons" for collaborative work.

We believe the best spaces (and those that generate the best team dynamics and results) include both types of space.

Identity and Ownership

There are two loose rules when trying to guide and determine what teams work on. First, work with the business, the Chief Product Owner, and the product team to decompose the business products/ projects into a meaningful set of focused themes.

Then, staff the teams to align with these product backlog themes. Clearly, each stream gets a Product Owner. Not only do we want the team to be staffed to successfully deliver on the business expectations, we want the backlog stream to enable a team identity and end-to-end ownership of the work. They should own the maintenance, feature development, technical evolution, and future release roadmap for their product or feature area.

Giving each team a sense of holistic identity and ownership is key to establishing team empowerment and ownership and ultimately delivering great results.

To summarize, there are a few primary approaches you can take to enable great teams:

1. Build the teams with knowledgeable, capable and self-directed people.

2. Keep the team together for as long as possible in both duration of time and co-location of space.

3. Encourage full participation while limiting part-time team members to those with specialty skills.

4. Keep the team size smaller, in the 6–8 person range, knowing they will be more effective than a larger group.

This advice isn't theoretical or academic. It's based on well documented experience in creating high-performance agile organizations and the realization of what works—and conversely, what does not.

Every Great Team Needs a Great Coach

When we think of great teams in sports, we typically attribute their success to the players who have superior ability to execute and to the head coach who helped develop the team and their skills and ultimately position them for great success. No one who follows sports believes that players and teams can go it alone without the coach—and certainly never the other way around.

Why then, when we discuss organizational agility, do we think teams, as talented as they may be, can go it alone without their day-to-day coach—their Scrum Master? Unfortunately, this role can be the most controversial of all in Scrum, and people who are not completely familiar with the Scrum roles sometimes react with confusion, suspicion, or outright incredulity. What does this even mean? What is this *master of Scrum*? Sounds like complete rubbish, an imaginary role that offers no credibility or substance.

Clearly, they need some help understanding the role of the Scrum Master.

A Scrum Master is the coach and day-to-day leader for the Scrum team, Product Owner (PO), and organization. Like the head coach in football, they promote and support the team by teaching values, theory, practices, and rules—effectively the foundations of success. Scrum Masters serve the Scrum team by shielding them from outside forces, removing impediments, and coaching them in self-organization and cross-functionality, all of which allows them to focus on creating high-value products. The Scrum Master also encourages the team to improve its development process and practices to make the next sprint more effective and enjoyable. They help keep the team focused on the sprint commitments.

Scrum Masters serve the PO by offering techniques for effective product backlog management; ensuring everyone understands the goals, scope, and product domain; and facilitating Scrum events as requested or needed. The organization relies on the Scrum Master to lead and coach the Scrum adoption, induce change to increase the productivity of the Scrum teams, and help everyone to understand and enact Scrum and empirical product development. In addition, Scrum Masters continually monitor transparency by inspecting the artifacts, sensing patterns, listening closely, and detecting differences between expected and real results.

Without the Scrum Master, we must assume that the Scrum team and PO work together like a well-oiled machine and fully comprehend expectations. (We have yet to experience this.) Who is going to help those outside the team understand which interactions are helpful and which aren't? Who will explain the *why* behind the *what* and the *how*? Who is monitoring the health of the team, keeping Scrum events focused and efficient, and coaching the team on autonomy, cross-functionality, and self-organization? Who is continually observing the team dynamics, enforcing the agile mindset, and challenging for continual improvement? More simply said, who is going to connect the team with its most effective path to success?

An additional way Scrum Masters can reinforce the value of the collaborative coaching view is by holding regular one-on-ones. These individual meetings are a chance to receive feedback and answer questions about Scrum and, more importantly, to develop the proper collaborative relationship with each team member. Spending one-on-one time with each person on the team sends the message that they, their thoughts, and their actions are valuable. This enables the Scrum Master to build trust, which is **key** for high performance.

A one-on-one session is an extremely efficient technique to:

- Connect with people
- Uncover impediments
- Learn of problems early on
- Provide space for feedback and coaching
- Teach the Scrum framework
- Gain insight into how the Scrum Master can improve

This technique is not only useful for team members. Scrum Masters can also schedule regular one-on-ones with the managers of their team members—not as a complaint session or an opportunity to air dirty laundry, but to establish a partnership where both roles are helping each team member, and the overall team, be the best they can be. This also helps the manager increase the effectiveness of their own one-on-ones with team members.

It's a lot like individual coaching for the players, in addition to coaching for the team as a group.

We don't always need to resort to sports analogies, but what if we rename the role of Scrum Master to Team Coach? Does that help turn on a mental light bulb? Do facial expressions loosen, eyebrows relax, and people lean forward, fingers steepled at their lips, in a pose of thoughtfulness?

So, perhaps that's it. If leadership and team members viewed Scrum Masters as coaches, then perhaps Scrum Masters wouldn't be continually trying to understand or justify their role.

After all, at work as in sports, every great team needs a coach. Don't they?

Self-Directed and Self-Organizing

One of the core principles of agile is the notion of a self-directed, self-managed, and self-organizing team. This is the foundation of moving rapid decision-making to the experts who know the details of the product best.

It's one of the hardest things to get right in team evolution efforts.

Often, we see one of two extremes. At one extreme, the teams use the mantra of self-organization and self-direction to avoid accountability. They can choose to do whatever they wish, whenever they wish, under the banner of "don't bother us, we're being agile."

The other extreme is when the management team says that they're empowering self-directed teams but doesn't change their own behavior. These leaders end up doing what they've always done—they tell folks what to do.

Self-directed teams, once given a mission or goal, are expected to sort out the challenges and deliver.

While this is a central notion in agile, it's often hard to get individuals and teams to embrace it. It's a compelling premise: you own your destiny (results), so figure things out. But people often fight this.

Is it a lack of practice in decision-making? Is it a fear of accountability? Is it a fear of failure?

It could be all three and much more.

It seems that many of us have become comfortable complaining about things and pointing upward to "them" as being the problem. Many individuals have become comfortable being told what to do. When the accountability resides with their managers, they are simply doing as they're told. However, if agile is done well, then "they" becomes "us," which can be scary.

On the flip side of this, when individuals and teams embrace self-direction, it's a magical thing. There is a shared accountability between the leadership team and the teams doing the work. It's balanced and effective, with each one supporting and trusting the other.

But this balance can often be quite difficult to achieve.

A Balanced Approach

The *Scrum Guide* describes the overall Scrum team this way:

> The Scrum Team consists of a Product Owner, the Development Team, and a Scrum Master. Scrum Teams are self-organizing and cross-functional. Self-organizing teams choose how best to accomplish their work, rather than being directed by others outside the team. Cross-functional teams have all competencies needed to accomplish the work without depending on others not part of the team. The team model in Scrum is designed to optimize flexibility, creativity, and productivity.[3]

It goes on to say the following about the development team:

> The Development Team consists of professionals who do the work of delivering a potentially releasable Increment of "Done" product at the end of each Sprint. Only members of the Development Team create the Increment. Development Teams are structured and empowered by the organization to organize and manage their own work. The resulting synergy

---

3 Schwaber and Sutherland, "The Scrum Guide," 6.

optimizes the Development Team's overall efficiency and effectiveness. Development Teams have the following characteristics:

- They are self-organizing. No one (not even the Scrum Master) tells the Development Team how to turn Product Backlog into Increments of potentially releasable functionality.

- Development Teams are cross-functional, with all of the skills as a team necessary to create a product Increment.[4]

In discussing self-organization, the *Scrum Guide* focuses on how the team decides to attack the work they've been asked to perform via the backlog. Schwaber and Sutherland go to great lengths to emphasize that the team owns and decides work strategy. They also emphasize a blending of roles to the point where they are near meaningless. The key points are team, teamwork, delivery of a product increment, and accountability.

In July 2011, Esther Derby published an article on her website addressing "Misconceptions about Self-Directed Teams":

1. Self-organizing teams are completely autonomous, self-managing, and don't need managers.

2. All you need to do to form a self-organizing team is provide a goal and apply pressure.

3. Since the team is self-organizing, they can accommodate moving people on and off the team easily.

On the management side, her article discusses an overall misconception surrounding the relationship or "dance" between the self-organizing team and the leadership structure within the organization (sometimes referred to as "management").

---

4 Schwaber and Sutherland, "The Scrum Guide," 7.

In most cases, there isn't a whole lot of guidance coming from the agile community around managing/leading agile teams. And usually what does come out emphasizes the team over management—management is basically told to "leave the team alone" or "go and handle a few impediments" as their primary role.

The management role Derby describes is balanced (and necessary).

> Like all teams, self-organizing teams need a compelling goal, skills, information, and enough time to form and perform, and they still need managers to create a supportive context, set appropriate boundaries and constraints, and connect the team to the organization.

Establishing Constraints

There seem to be two schools of thought when it comes to applying constraints to agile teams. One is that constraints are inherently bad, undermining the empowerment and accountability of the teams. We sometimes see this in agile coaches who use terms like *agile purism*, *un-agile*, *un-lean*, *arbitrary*, *dogmatic*, *prescriptive*, or *prescription* to describe anything that "forces" the team to do something against their will. These coaches want the team to be unencumbered in their journey, with literally *no* constraints. Organizational leaders should avoid this type of coaching—it is likely going to be at odds with achieving meaningful results in product delivery.

Unless you're working in your own company, or perhaps for a nonprofit, it's hard to imagine a job (yes, agile team members usually work) with a total lack of constraints. Usually there are several:

- Quality constraints
- Appropriate working conditions (language, dress, hours, etc.)
- Business and financial constraints
- Agile constraints like Definition of Done, agile approaches used, and tooling

- Legal constraints

But as we're applying constraints, we need to be careful that they're not too oppressive. They need to leave some room for the team to make their own rules and their own decisions.

Definition of Done is an example. We believe teams need a deep and broad Definition of Done, but at the same time, we usually encourage teams to extend their Definition of Done with team-based agreements and to make it their own.

We encourage the same thing when the team is making other operational agreements among themselves.

Creating Self-Organizing Teams

So, with all this in mind, how do we create self-organizing teams?

This is likely not something we can just do. The leadership team has a responsibility to create a fertile space for these sorts of teams to form, become established, and grow.

1. Staff the team with the skills required to deliver on their backlog.

2. Avoid part-time team members at all costs. If you do have some, limit them and clearly define their capacity within the team.

3. If you're doing Scrum, have a dedicated Product Owner and Scrum Master. Make sure they have the experience, time, and focus to do the job well.

4. Respect the autonomy of the team and trust them to deliver on your stated goals and directives.

5. Engage in all aspects of the agile ceremonies so that you leverage the transparency and real-time adjustment inherent to the methods.

The team has self-direction responsibilities as well:

1. Hold each other accountable to professional ethics and standards.

2. Have congruent discussions in retrospectives, guiding the team towards continuous improvement.

3. Have the courage to push back as appropriate on traditional leadership that might be pushing the team too hard or in the wrong direction.

4. Hold quality dear within the team, not only from a Definition of Done perspective, but with solid professional attitudes and practices.

5. Work together respectfully (swarming around the work) delivering as many high-quality products as possible.

Section 4

Leading Transformations

Agile Transformation Teams

Leading an organizational shift to agile requires alignment of the entire team, top to bottom. This means the leadership team must take an active and obvious role in leading this change. One of the core challenges for most leaders is that they are stuck telling their teams and organizations "this needs to shift to enable a successful conversion to agile," as opposed to actively participating in the transformation. That is, they are not walking their talk. This can cause substantial damage to the move to agility.

This is usually not a malicious or lazy play. It's simply that leadership team members have more important things to do—things that require their specific skill set and expertise—so there is little to no time left for working like or with their agile teams.

Some may think this is OK and that it doesn't affect the agile organization (or the potential agile organization). I think it has a very negative effect.

An organizational Agile Transformation Team can help.

The agile Transformation Team is formed to establish and guide the agile journey within an organization. It's usually made up of internal senior leaders and internal or external coaches and agile change agents. The key attributes of the group are a passion for agile principles and a vision for the organization.

The team's entire focus is transformation, at both the strategic level and the tactical/execution level. Often, these teams are larger than the Scrum guidance suggests—as many as ten or twelve people. While this might be unwieldy, the advantage is usually broader organizational representation.

To start, the Agile Transformation Team is organized like any other agile team. Let's use Scrum as an example. Often the Transformation Team is formed as a Scrum team.

There is a Scrum Master—usually one of the more seasoned agilists within the organization. This person needs strong skills as a facilitator and should be a well-versed Scrum Master.

The Transformation Team Product Owner (PO) is usually the most senior leader chartered with leading the effort. In this case, the "product" is the agile transformation.

The core team is composed of representatives from the overall organization. Often it includes:

- CIO, CTO, CPO, CMO, etc.
- Technical leaders at the VP and director level
- Development leaders
- QA and Test leaders
- Product leaders
- Project (PMO) leaders
- Business analysis and UX leaders
- Tooling (admin, DevOps, etc.) leaders
- Architectural leaders

The Transformation Team's membership is not always static. Membership in the team can fluctuate in the first few sprints as members figure out their capacity, roles, and interactions. For instance, someone may join the team for a specific initiative (epic, story, focus point) and then leave after it's complete.

Sometimes the roles shift as well. For example, some Transformation Teams rotate the role of Scrum Master across the team on some interval, perhaps monthly.

The team operates as a "real" Scrum team. That is, they:

- Form and establish norms, create a Definition of Done, and agree on tooling/practices.
- Agree on sprint length and meeting timing.
- Create a backlog together. It doesn't have to be perfect at the beginning, just good enough for one or two sprints to "prime the pump."
- Perform initial and ongoing backlog refinement, initially focused on the first sprint.
- Plan and execute sprints, with daily stand-ups.
- Deliver results in sprint demos.
- Hold retrospectives and aim to continuously improve.

One of the most interesting aspects of this leadership team is that they participate in the practices they are promoting for the teams and team members they manage. They also practice within the same agile team dynamics and expectations. For example, it is almost universally true that these teams bite off too much work in their first few sprints and fail to deliver on their sprint goals. This is a great lesson for the leadership team. It brings them into the real world that their teams live in every day.

Once formed and practicing, the Transformation Team becomes the hub for all organizational activity related to the overall transformation.

Even though the team makeup looks similar, the Transformation Team's work makes it quite different from a Scrum team. This team's work is more strategic, focused on establishing vision, mission, and overarching goals and the plan to meet the goals. Their work is focused more on communication and transparency, removing impediments and providing resources. They are focused on initiatives, goals, and objectives, often establishing acceptance criteria for each story (to measure interim and final closure) while focusing on the overall metrics for the organization. Quite often, the work of this team activates, engages, or delegates to others throughout the organization.

Still, they are accountable and responsible for delivering the work they plan.

One of the more interesting aspects of the Agile Transformation Team is the true, collaborative, pairing-based teamwork it engenders across the members.

Often, this is the first time that this group has worked together as part of a unified and aligned team. Expect some turbulence as they figure out how to work together and balance across their organizational roles vs. their transformation-based roles.

Patrick Lencioni's *Five Dysfunctions of a Team* (Jossey-Bass, 2002) can help the group establish the conditions for high-performance and trust-based teaming. It's a quick read and quite useful.

One of the most critical responsibilities of the Transformation Team is creating a path to success for the organizational agile rollout. This is typically accomplished by identifying the preferred path of the rollout. Leaders often want to get going a bit faster than the organization can digest and opt for some sort of Big Bang or rapid rollout. A better approach may be identifying a few pilot or proof of concept teams to begin and learn with. This can help the organization learn how it might best digest the changes associated with this new way of working.

Step 1 is to identify the pilot projects and teams, inclusive of all roles in the Scrum team—PO, Scrum Master, and dedicated team members. The team should be trained together, which is highly effective and gets them rolling on being successful as a group. This training should also include the Agile Coach assigned to the team. If you want to jump-start the PO and Scrum Master, having them attend specialized role training can be quite effective.

Once the pilot teams are executing, likely in a Scrum pattern to start, identify the outcomes each team is shooting for and some metrics to help track maturation of the teams in this new way of working.

While the pilots are executing, the Transformation Leaders should be developing a roadmap for the long-term rollout. A pattern that can be effective is to rollout to teams that the pilots are dependent on, which likely catches all the teams in a fairly logical pattern. This means that each team identifies the 2–4 teams they are most dependent on and the Transformation Team uses that information to roll out waves of teams following the same team formation, training, and coaching model used for the pilot teams.

One of the biggest factors the Transformation Leaders need to be aware of is the impact of change.

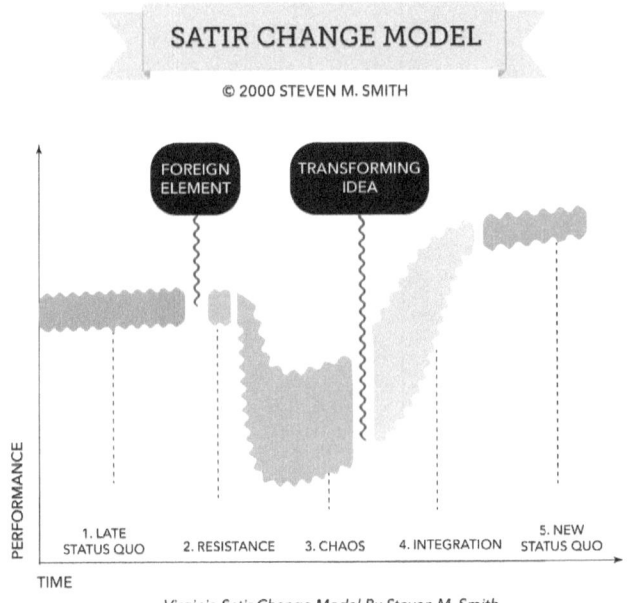

Figure 3. The Satir Change Model. Even well-planned changes introduce some chaos that will impact productivity until the organization adjusts. Reproduced by permission from Steven M. Smith, [source]

When a change agent is introduced, there is an initial drop in productivity due to the chaos created by the change (Figure 3). The dueling metrics approach described later in this section will identify how the teams are maturing and how effective they are becoming. A speed-related metric, perhaps velocity or velocity index, and a quality-related metric, perhaps defects observed, can be used to analyze how teams are progressing.

The Agile Transformation Team is vital to the rollout of agile. Leaders need to lead by example and to walk in the same shoes as their teams. When they do, we see highly successful agile transformations. When leadership pushes a "team only" approach, rollout failure is much more common than success.

Encourage Everyone to Lead

In agile organizations and teams, we continue to teach the importance of emphasizing leadership over management and teamwork over individual accomplishments. What intentional actions are we taking to achieve this vital goal?

We should create an environment in which every person has a chance to lead in some way, every day. Further, we should be encouraging continuous leadership behavior by every team member. Great ideas and leadership behaviors are not the exclusive property of senior leaders, and, in mature agile organizations, there is an evolution of team member leadership responsibility.

Admired leaders begin with a team-first mentality:

- We before me
- Culture of innovation
- Empowerment of everyone
- Obsession with client success

These attributes have rung true with us for years now and seem to resonate with other leaders as well. One team reminded of these traits built a Leadership Compass depicting their leadership North Star.

Figure 4. Leadership Compass illustrating key elements of a team-first outlook on leadership

One way to develop great leadership skills is to model our behavior after leaders who are widely admired. These are people who find a way to bring the best version of themselves daily and continually develop leadership characteristics in everyone around them. One incredible leader we worked with was terrific at delivering feedback in a constructive and humble way. She was a truly extraordinary relationship builder who always found time to mentor anyone who sought her advice. We were continually amazed at her ability to balance an incredible workload and busy family life and still find time to help others reach their maximum potential. She demonstrated that at the center of great leadership is a deep caring for people and the extension of trust. Her behavior showed that leadership is not assigned—it is earned and continually learned!

In highly effective organizations, everyone needs to lead regularly. That leadership can come in many forms: sharing knowledge and information, setting a great example of teamwork, or simply extending trust. Leading through influence and motivation is a much more powerful form of leadership than being appointed. When we are appointed, people in our teams may feel obligated to agree with us and to pursue our agenda, even if they disagree. When there is no direct report correlation, we need to find other ways to connect, influence, and motivate. Leading through influence causes us to appreciate everyone's point of view and empowerment. When we leverage all team members' strengths to develop better solutions, everyone gets better and we as leaders learn to become force multipliers.

One leading financial services firm asked employees to model the following behaviors. Ask yourselves if you demonstrate these approaches:

- Be obsessed with what is best for the customer.
- Tell it like it is and hear it as intended.
- Value pace over perfection and encourage risk-taking.
- Create an environment in which people can reach their maximum potential.
- Empower team decision-making.
- Think and work across the organization.
- Own the results.

An example of a leader with some phenomenal behavior worth modeling is former U.S. Navy Captain David Marquet. His story illustrates leadership courage while building an environment in which everyone showed leadership every day. Inno-Versity's illustrated adaptation of Marquet's speech "Greatness" is available on YouTube and well worth the ten minutes.

The ultimate focus of great leadership is creating an environment in which teams and team members can achieve their maximum potential. What better way to demonstrate that than to encourage leadership everywhere!

Be Disruptive!

Agile transformations are about making agile habits stick while finding new and better ways to achieve results. When we start these transformations, we often begin with the basic values of the Agile Manifesto.

Individuals and interactions over processes and tools

Working software over comprehensive documentation

Customer collaboration over contract negotiation

Responding to change over following a plan

From these powerful basics, we tend to try to deploy agile frameworks to "get the transformation going." This can lead us to initially define our transformation as getting good at the following:

- Scrum or Kanban
- Daily stand-ups
- Building backlogs
- Having meaningful retrospectives
- Maybe scaling our agility in some way

This does typically lead to important gains, but we should challenge ourselves with more:

1. Are these gains evolutionary or revolutionary?
2. Do these gains represent all the achievements possible?

3. Are these changes sewn into the fabric of the organization, or are they only temporary?

Along the way to building truly agile organizations, we get good at one or more of the frameworks, but we don't implement the fundamental cultural changes needed to make the new mindset last. We also sometimes lose focus on what success looks like. We might start measuring the number of Scrum teams created, the successful training of our associate teams, or the introduction of new tools like Jira to build backlogs. These are important steps, but perhaps not as important as achieving groundbreaking outcomes like moving applications to the cloud or mobilization of all application offerings.

This is not to trivialize the initial gains achieved through the new habits of these frameworks. They are great, but focusing on frameworks can limit our true transformation capability if we don't challenge ourselves further. The true power of agility is in the ability to create an organization that, at its core, continuously challenges itself to be better, to reach higher, and to be dissatisfied with the status quo—whatever it has become or evolved into.

In a word, we need to build organizations that "disrupt" themselves—forever!

The role of an agile organizational leader is to model continuous organizational disruption and demonstrate the behavior of never being OK with the status quo.

By mentoring others and creating an environment of healthy discontent and continuous, constructive challenge, we set our overall culture to a pattern of continuous, constructive change. This type of culture fundamentally aims to never be satisfied with the current:

- Time to market
- Quality of product
- Team dynamics
- Skills and capabilities

- Competitive product advantages
- Market share

This doesn't mean we don't celebrate milestones and victories of achievement. It does mean that once we have achieved a goal, and perhaps launched a new product or application, the new target is to make that irrelevant and supplant it with the next newer and better version that our customers celebrate. Our customers have ever-evolving objectives and needs. A culture of continuous disruption and healthy dissatisfaction with the status quo may be the best way to meet that challenge!

What are you willing to disrupt next?

Grit: The Secret Ingredient

Traditional views indicate that there are two keys to achieving organizational agility: a well-formed implementation of training followed by coaching and top-line organizational support. While that is the obvious answer, and correct, our observation is that scrappiness and grit are vital to agile success. A transformational move to agile is typically not smooth. It is tough work!

In the opening weeks of an agile rollout, excitement, support, and momentum build up. Everyone is passionate about this new endeavor and the seemingly endless positive organizational change about to occur. Leadership is excited about this new and fantastic vehicle to deliver new products on time or ahead of time and at a reduced cost. The team members feel great about their training and the new levels of empowerment headed their way. What could go wrong?

One organization we recently observed was having some difficulty. This company wanted agile to be the path to future greatness and organizational harmony. They announced the transformation as the new and better way of working. After a few weeks, the agile coaches raised several potential impediments to success in team and leadership behaviors.

When they delivered this message, leadership pushed back. They asserted the list of recommended improvements would be "too disruptive." They did not want to make these extensive changes; the people doing the work would push back because it would be too difficult. We explained that a move to true agility was not going to be as simple as "having some daily meetings." They would need grit and determination, but it was clear that the leaders themselves wanted little to do with personal transformation. We told them they would have to grind through the changes or face the reality that they would likely fail.

The good news is that after a few more candid discussions the leaders and teams embraced the changes they needed to make. Additionally, as a result of those conversations, they decided that grit was a vital ingredient they needed to be successful and started having open conversations about this characteristic. They understood that knowing the agile vocabulary and approach would not be enough to turn the ship.

We talk about the discipline required to be successful in agile. It looks so easy, but it can be so hard! It takes long-term energy, determination, and a willingness to break through new barriers to achieve the goals. Success does not happen overnight; it often takes several months to see gains that become genuinely groundbreaking. Countless organizations have tried and failed because they were unwilling to sustain the time and energy commitment needed to make the changes stick.

Once the halo effect of the first few weeks of agile transformation wears off, organizations who, through dogged determination, continue fighting the good fight will find themselves rewarded. Passing through the stages of forming and storming to get to norming and maybe even performing requires grit: courage, perseverance, and resilience. In the words of Angela Duckworth, people with grit "don't believe that failure is a permanent condition."[5] Duckworth further asserts that nearly every change, no matter how difficult, can be made to work. If your organization has grit, studies show that you are well aligned for success in your agile transformation initiative.

---

5 Angela Duckworth, *Grit: The Power of Passion and Perseverance* (Simon & Schuster, 2016).

Using Dueling Metrics

Analytics have become a central focus of digital technology transformations in the past few years. These complex days of rapid technological evolution have many businesses questioning how to best measure success. This pursuit of analytics has also prompted a conversation about *one metric that matters* (OMTM). We think the OMTM conversation is popular because leadership tends to want each of their favorite metrics involved in the success definition. That results in seven to ten metrics of success and a list something like this:

- Sprint success
- Sprint burn down
- Velocity
- Escaped defects
- Build success
- Cycle time
- Sprint scope change
- Team happiness
- Team member turnover
- And on and on and on

This list is too unwieldy to track, manage, or learn from, yet from this list we ask teams to judge their output and outcomes and then find ways to improve. This type of overwhelming measurement prompts teams to reduce those metrics and look to the theory of OMTM, which is often seen as the one magic metric to get everyone off their collective backs.

Companies can use too many metrics, or not enough. At one client, the pursuit of metrics and measures became the single biggest impediment of the team. Several execs insisted on their own favorites and wanted frequent reports about those metrics. The Scrum Master and Product Owner were so consumed with reporting on these metrics that it became their full-time jobs. Very little attention was being paid to the backlog or the current sprint, so the team's progress ground to a halt.

In another case, a team got so entwined searching for the perfect OMTM that they measured nothing at all—they could not find the single metric that encompassed everything they needed.

The pursuit of analytics should not be that consuming. The reinforcement of metric-driven continuous improvement is at the heart of this recommendation: find a handful of useful measures and use them to improve!

We support greatly reduced measures and metrics, but have seen OMTM cause some bad habits due to its potential for oversimplification. Plainly, success in a single metric can cause teams to focus and behave too myopically and potentially ineffectively.

Instead, we propose an amendment to OMTM. Let's call it **dueling metrics**. In this approach, we pick two metrics that have natural friction with each other, causing teams to build better habits, improve more obviously, and deliver better outcomes.

As an example, consider *velocity* competing with *escaped defects* or *cycle time* competing with *sprint scope changes*. In the first example, moving faster (velocity) without deep concern for quality (escaped defects) does not serve a team or its customers well. Concurrent success in these two metrics is difficult—and that is the point. We should promote the pursuit of balance in our approach to metrics, which leads to higher-performing teams with better long-term habits.

We want teams to build great habits. Using dueling metrics, teams are challenged to be much better in their habits, actions, and outcomes.

Conclusion

Sustaining Agility in an Increasingly Complex World

As organizations continue to move to new and evolving ways to serve customers, businesses need to be nimbler and more responsive than ever. Mobile apps, cloud computing, DevOps, and data analytics are just some of the new and demanding trends we all must manage in this increasingly digital world. Every part of every business is being challenged to accelerate change in ways they could not imagine a few years ago.

To achieve that responsiveness, we need to shift our models of product delivery. Agile and end-to-end organizational agility are tried and true methods of doing this. This book explores the four patterns we believe are essential to unleashing organizational agility so teams can get things done reliably and to become predictable in that completion.

First, apply agile approaches and concepts to get things done. By setting the stage with thorough organizational agility methods, we can identify smaller chunks of work to complete quickly and predictably. We can see what work is the highest priority and, maybe more importantly, identify what will not get any attention, focus, or energy—for now. By limiting how much is getting done at any one time we enable the completion of high-value and heavily demanded work, which becomes the foundation for great customer relationships. Customers want completed products delivered—not activity!

Second, build a strong understanding and support of agile throughout the organization's senior leadership team. Ensuring that leaders go first sets the tone for how these new approaches will be adopted and raises the likelihood that the needed top-down cultural shift is in place. Nothing builds teams better than fully engaged and supportive leaders. Nothing kills a change in approach more than a mentality that says "this is good for you, but not necessarily for me!"

Third, lay the foundation for teams to become high performance and to enjoy repeated success. Have approaches in place to ensure teams are built with team members who all have great attitudes. Positive energy can overcome nearly any obstacle. Have a plan to get training, mentoring, and coaching in place to assure a focus on continuous improvement. Finally, give teams and team members the space they need to make their own decisions and solve their own problems. Remember, they are the experts of their domains and have more information than anyone else to guide clarity in those decisions.

Last, but certainly not least, agile transformations take time, effort, and engaged leadership. Having a well-constructed and attended Agile Transformation Team enables the entire organization to have a game plan for the cultural shift required. Agile transformations are at their core disruptive. Embrace the disruption and make it work in your favor. Nothing kills organizational gains better than clinging to the status quo. Introducing change in a constructive manner sets the stage for ongoing improvements. Managing that change with metrics also helps keep the transformation on track. Don't fall in love with a single measurement. Know that people react to how they are being measured, keep at least two equal and opposite measures in place, and consider changing what you measure periodically to help teams continue to evolve and improve.

Achieving successful change often requires grit. Have the sheer determination to be successful and to not allow anything to stand in the way of that success. The new and better way of working will take time to shape and take hold.

Be ready for the road ahead; it can be tough and will certainly bring unanticipated situations and challenges. As you progress, your team members, teams, and leaders—and, most importantly, your customers—will achieve higher levels of success and satisfaction than you previously thought possible!

www.ingramcontent.com/pod-product-compliance
Lightning Source LLC
Chambersburg PA
CBHW020603220526
45463CB00006B/2434